Out and About

Greg Roza

NEIGHBORHOOD READERS

Rosen Classroom Books & Materials™

New York

We walk to the park.

← PARK

We walk to the store.

Mary's Store

We walk to the zoo.

ZOO

We walk home.